The American Dream:
Coming to the United States

by Lana Cruce

PEARSON

Scott
Foresman

Editorial Offices: Glenview, Illinois • Parsippany, New Jersey • New York, New York
Sales Offices: Needham, Massachusetts • Duluth, Georgia • Glenview, Illinois
Coppell, Texas • Ontario, California • Mesa, Arizona

ISBN: 0-328-13385-X

7 8 9 10 V0G1 14 13 12 11 10 09 08

Immigrants are people who leave the countries where they were born and then move to other countries to make new homes. Most of the people who live in the United States are related to immigrants or are immigrants themselves.

The United States is sometimes called a nation of immigrants, or a "melting pot." The population of the United States is a mix of people from countries all over the world. Many people believe that immigration has made the United States the strong nation that it is today.

The United States became a nation because many people came here to start a new and better life.

Even the earliest people to live in what is now the United States were immigrants. Ancestors of Native Americans came from Siberia, a country in Asia. They came to what is now the state of Alaska. Slowly they migrated, or moved, south. They settled in many areas of North America and South America.

Siberia

Asia

Alaska

North America

South America

Today, about one million people immigrate to the United States every year. Their journeys may take many days. Often, families must sleep overnight in airports on their way.

Immigrant families look forward to living in the United States.

People come to the United States for many reasons. They may come because there are not enough jobs in their native countries. They believe that they will earn more money in the United States to support their families.

This woman is very happy to become an American citizen.

People may immigrate to the United
States because living conditions in their home
countries are poor. Cities may be too crowded.
There may not be enough food or clean water
for everyone.

These people live in poor conditions in Cairo, Egypt.

Some people come to the United States to give their children a better education. Maybe they could not pay to send their children to school in their native countries. Or maybe the schools there were not good. In the United States, public schools promise a free and equal education for all children.

Education is one reason people immigrate to the United States.

Many people come to the United States seeking freedom. There may be war and violence in their native countries. Families may be in danger if they mention their opinions. They may not be allowed to practice religion.

The Statue of Liberty is a symbol of hope and freedom to immigrants.

Many famous Americans are immigrants. Arnold Schwarzenegger came to the United States from Austria. He was twenty-one years old. He became a popular actor. Then, in 2003, he was elected governor of California.

Patrick Ewing is an admired basketball player. He came to the United States from Jamaica when he was about twelve years old.

Patrick Ewing immigrated to the U.S. from Jamaica.

The United States would be very different without immigration. Immigrants bring many customs and traditions with them to the United States. American culture is a twist of many cultures braided together. Think of how much Americans can learn from each other!

These children are having fun making music in a Fourth of July parade.